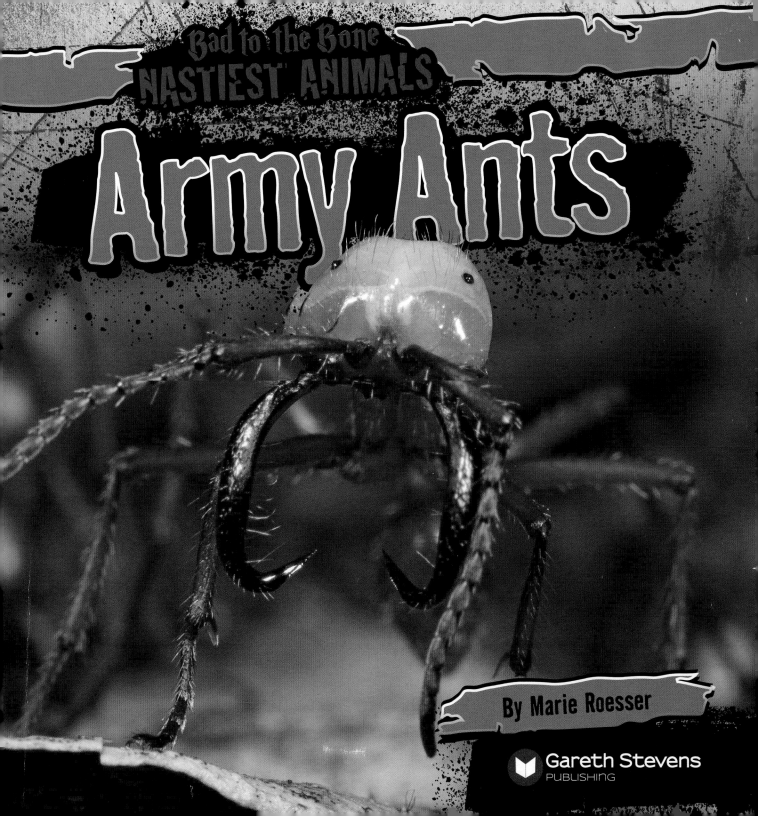

Bad to the Bone
NASTIEST ANIMALS

Army Ants

By Marie Roesser

Gareth Stevens
PUBLISHING

Please visit our website, www.garethstevens.com. For a free color catalog of all our high-quality books, call toll free 1-800-542-2595 or fax 1-877-542-2596.

Library of Congress Cataloging-in-Publication Data

Roesser, Marie, author.
 Army ants / Marie Roesser.
      pages cm. — (Bad to the bone. Nastiest animals)
 Includes bibliographical references and index.
 ISBN 978-1-4824-1950-4 (pbk.)
 ISBN 978-1-4824-1949-8 (6 pack)
 ISBN 978-1-4824-1951-1 (library binding)
 1. Army ants—Juvenile literature. I. Title.
 QL568.F7R64 2015
 595.79'6—dc23

                                    2014020523

First Edition

Published in 2015 by
Gareth Stevens Publishing
111 East 14th Street, Suite 349
New York, NY 10003

Copyright © 2015 Gareth Stevens Publishing

Designer: Michael Flynn
Editor: Therese Shea

Photo credits: Cover, p. 1 Piotr Naskrecki/Minden Pictures/Getty Images; cover, pp. 1–24 (series art) foxie/Shutterstock.com; cover, pp. 1–24 (series art) Larysa Ray/Shutterstock.com; cover, pp. 1–24 (series art) LeksusTuss/Shutterstock.com; pp. 5, 17 Dr. Morley Read/Shutterstock.com; p. 7 ekler/Shutterstock.com; p. 9 Gregory MD./Photo Researchers/Getty Images; p. 11 Oxford Scientific/Getty Images; p. 13 Geoff Gallice from Gainesville, FL, USA/Wikipedia.com; p. 15 Rudolf Freund/Photo Researchers/Getty Images; p. 19 Gilbert M. Grosvenor/National Geographic/Getty Images; p. 21 Mdf/Wikipedia.com.

Printed in the United States of America

CPSIA compliance information: Batch #CW15GS: For further information contact Gareth Stevens, New York, New York at 1-800-542-2595.

Contents

Incredible Army 4

Hot Homes. 6

Body Builders. 8

The Queen and Her Colony. 10

Hard Workers. 12

Army Ant Young 14

Army Majors. 16

On the March. 18

Keystone Species 20

Glossary. 22

For More Information 23

Index 24

Words in the glossary appear in **bold** type the first time they are used in the text.

Incredible Army

Picture an animal covered with **armor** that has knifelike jaws. That's pretty scary, isn't it? It's a good thing the army ant, which has both of these **adaptations**, is so small. We don't need to be frightened of them.

However, working together, these ants are a hungry, unstoppable army feared by many animals. They can kill prey much larger than themselves. Army ants have earned their name by their large numbers as well as their **fierce** nature.

That's Nasty!

It's a good thing people don't come in contact with army ants often. They can sting!

The scientific name for the most commonly studied army ant is *Eciton burchellii*. It's also called Burchell's army ant. The facts in this book focus on this **species**.

Hot Homes

There are many, many species of army ants. As many as 200 species have been found so far. Most are located in the hot, **humid** rainforests of Central and South America. In other parts of the world, including Africa, they're called driver ants.

Army ants live in nests they build at the base of trees, under fallen logs, or inside hollow tree trunks. Army ants move to a new nest when they run out of food in one place.

That's Nasty!

Only two of the many species of army ants march in the **destructive** groups these ants are feared for.

North
America

Central
America

South
America

Burchell's army
ants range

Africa

This map shows the location of Burchell's army ants.
Some are even found north of Central America,
in the rainforests of Mexico.

Body Builders

Army ant nests are called bivouacs (BIH-vuh-waaks). The nests are actually *made* of ants! Army ants have hooks on their feet, which they use to grip each other. Their bodies form a roof over the army ant queen and her young.

When army ants are looking for food and there's a hole in their path, they fill it with their own bodies. This is so that other army ants can climb over and find food. Army ants don't let anything stop them from getting their food!

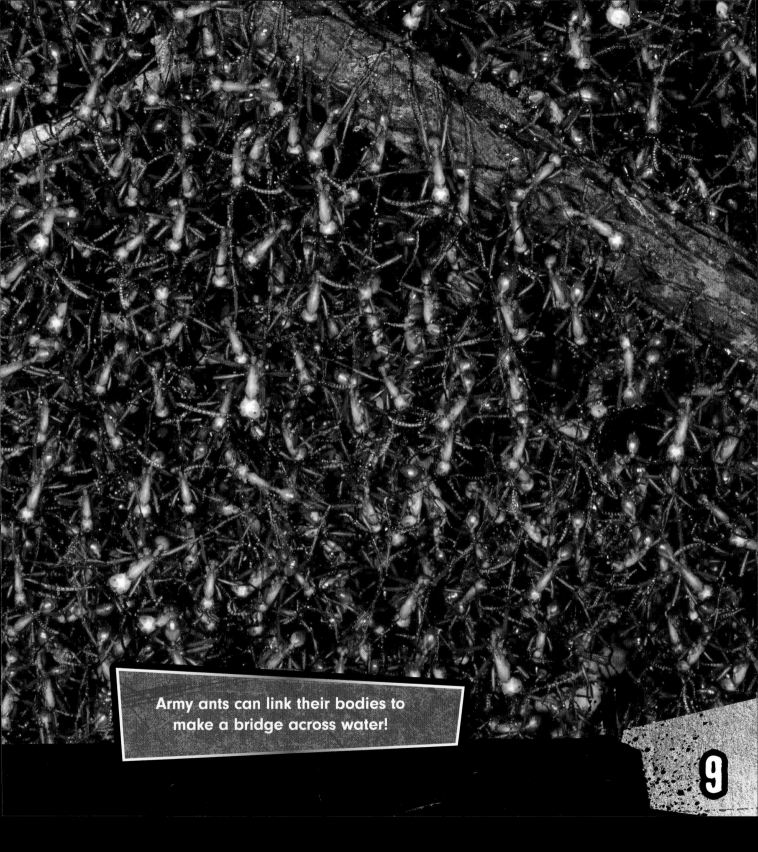

Army ants can link their bodies to make a bridge across water!

The Queen and Her Colony

Army ants live in groups called colonies. A colony may have more than 500,000 ants! Each colony has a queen whose job is to lay eggs. The queen is usually the only female. When the queen does produce a new queen ant, this young queen will **mate** and leave with some ants to form a new colony. The two colonies become enemies and may even fight each other!

Besides the queen, a colony is made up of smaller groups called castes (KASTS). Members of each caste perform a special role in the colony.

The queen army ant is the largest in the colony.
She can be up to 2 inches (5.1 cm) long.

Hard Workers

The workers are the smallest army ants. However, there are many of them in each colony. They take care of the colony's young. They also collect food and carry it back to the colony. They can do this even though they're blind! Workers produce **pheromones** (FEHR-uh-mohnz) to "talk" to each other.

Workers use sharp mouthparts, called mandibles, to cut up prey so it's easier to carry back to the nest. Prey include other ants, tarantulas, flies, termites, and insect eggs and **larvae**.

That's Nasty!

Worker ants chew food before feeding it to young ants.

Army ants will eat any animal, whether it's alive or dead! Here, they carry wasp larvae back to their nest.

Army Ant Young

The queen army ant lays up to 100,000 eggs at one time. The colony stays in the nest for about 20 days until the eggs hatch into larvae.

Workers try to keep up with feeding the hungry larvae, going out to gather food every day. The colony may have to move to a new nest each day to find enough. After about 15 days of this, larvae become **pupae**. Then the colony stays in one place until the pupae become adult army ants.

These army ant workers are moving the colony's pupae to a new nest.

Army Majors

There is also a caste in each army ant colony whose job is to guard the colony from enemies. These protectors are sometimes called soldiers or majors.

Army ant majors are larger than workers but smaller than the queen. They have a big head and very large, very sharp mandibles to help them fight. Some species of majors also have stingers, while others can spray a poisonous liquid at enemies. Ant majors help workers capture large prey, too.

That's Nasty!

Army ant mandibles are sharp like scissors!

Army ant majors are about 1 inch (2.5 cm) long.

On the March

When army ant workers are on the move to find food to bring back to the nest, they're called a raiding party. A party may travel more than 650 feet (200 m) from the nest during their raids. Raiding parties can stretch out to 100 feet (30 m) across and may include 200,000 workers! This may look a bit like a river of army ants.

The "river" captures insects, spiders, and other prey. The raiding party also kills animals that army ants don't eat but are in the way, such as lizards and snakes.

Army ants form lanes of ants when going out to search for food and returning to the nest.

Keystone Species

As many as 300 other species depend on army ants in some way. For example, many kinds of birds follow an army ant colony. When bugs and other animals run from the raiding party, the birds swoop down and take a bite.

Other animals, including beetles, wasps, and millipedes, can make themselves smell like army ants. So, they can travel with the colony and help themselves to prey.

For these reasons, army ants are called a keystone species. This means that these nasty animals are an essential part of their rainforest homes.

That's Nasty!

Butterflies follow birds that travel with army ants to eat the birds' droppings!

mandibles can cut and slice

can kill larger prey

Army Ants: So Nasty!

can make homes and bridges with their bodies

some sting or produce poisonous liquid

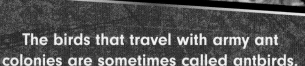

The birds that travel with army ant colonies are sometimes called antbirds.

Glossary

adaptation: a change in a type of animal that makes it better able to live in its surroundings

armor: a thick covering worn to keep someone or something safe from harm

destructive: causing great harm or damage

fierce: showing great toughness and a desire to fight

humid: having a high level of water in the air

larvae: bugs in an early life stage that have a wormlike form. The singular form is "larva."

mate: to come together to make babies

pheromone: matter made by an animal that can affect how other animals of the same species behave

pupae: bugs that are changing from larvae to adults, usually inside a case or cocoon. The singular form is "pupa."

species: a group of plants or animals that are all the same kind

For More Information

Books

Markle, Sandra. *Army Ants*. Minneapolis, MN: Lerner Publications, 2005.

Simon, Seymour. *Deadly Ants*. Mineola, NY: Dover Publications, 2012.

Twist, Clint. *The Life Cycle of Army Ants*. Mankato, MN: NewForest Press, 2013.

Websites

Army Ant
www.arkive.org/army-ant/eciton-burchellii/
Check out amazing videos and photos of army ants on this site.

Army Ant
www.bbc.co.uk/nature/life/Eciton_burchellii
Read many facts about the most famous species of army ants.

Index

Africa 6

armor 4

bivouacs 8

Burchell's army ant 5, 7

castes 10, 16

Central America 6, 7

colonies 10, 11, 12, 14, 15, 16,
    20, 21

eggs 10, 12, 14

food 6, 8, 12, 14, 18, 19

jaws 4

keystone species 20

larvae 12, 13, 14

majors 16, 17

mandibles 12, 16, 21

nests 6, 8, 12, 13, 14, 15, 18, 19

pheromones 12

poisonous liquid 16, 21

prey 4, 12, 16, 18, 20, 21

pupae 14, 15

queen 8, 10, 11, 14, 16

raiding party 18, 20

South America 6

species 5, 6, 16, 20

sting 4, 16, 21

workers 12, 14, 15, 16, 18